Christmas! Now with more Cat Butts!

What's a trimming of a tree, or a cup of hot cocoa, or a cozy night by the fire without the company of at least one cat butt?

Share the joys and traditions of the season with your favorite felines and their behinds in this holiday coloring concoction of Christmastime and Cat Butts!

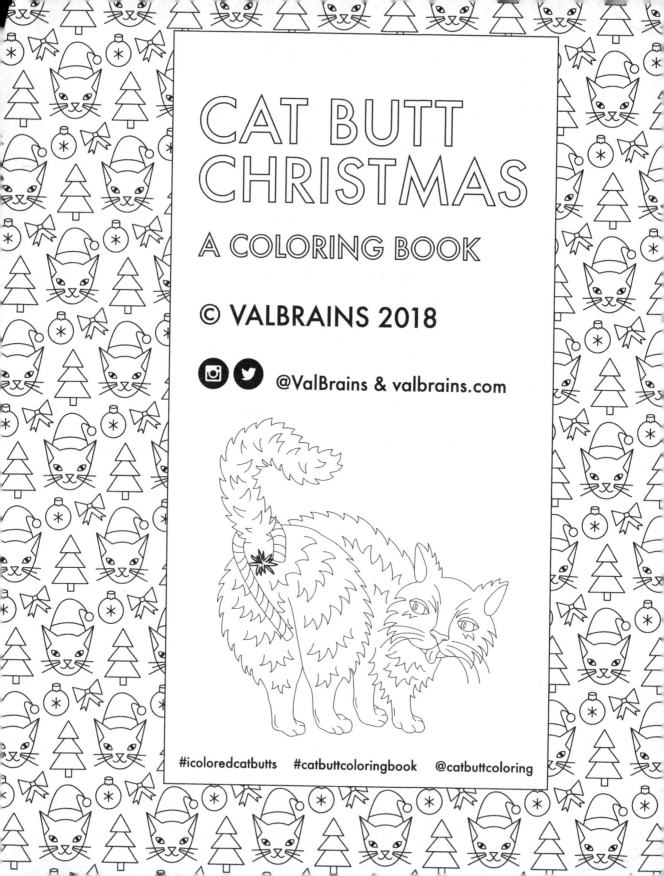

CAT BUTT CHRISTMAS

A COLORING BOOK

© VALBRAINS 2018

@ValBrains & valbrains.com

#icoloredcatbutts   #catbuttcoloringbook   @catbuttcoloring

UNDER THE MEOWSTLETOE

fold down

Colored by:

To:

fold up

POINSETTIA POSTERIOR

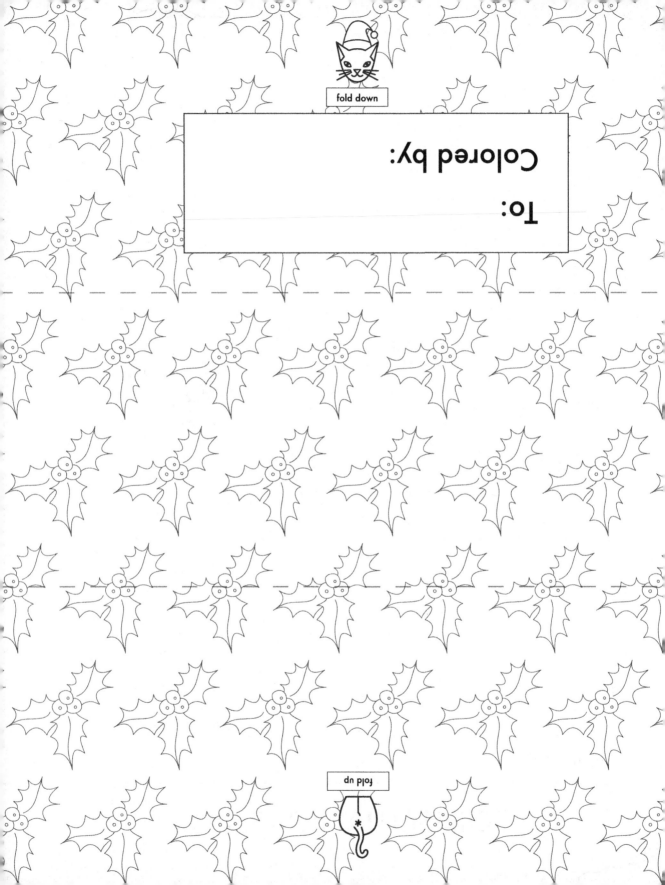

fold down

Colored by:

To:

fold up

CHIMNEY CHALLENGES

fold down

To:

Colored by:

fold up

GINGERBUTT COOKIES

fold down

To:

Colored by:

fold up

SNEAK CHEEK

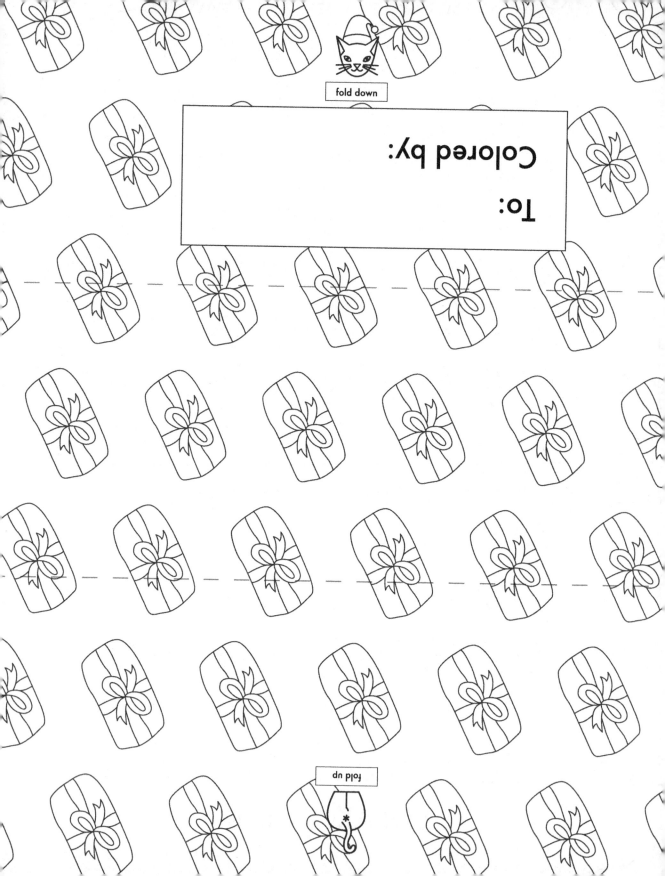

fold down

To:

Colored by:

fold up

CURIOUS CAT BUTTS

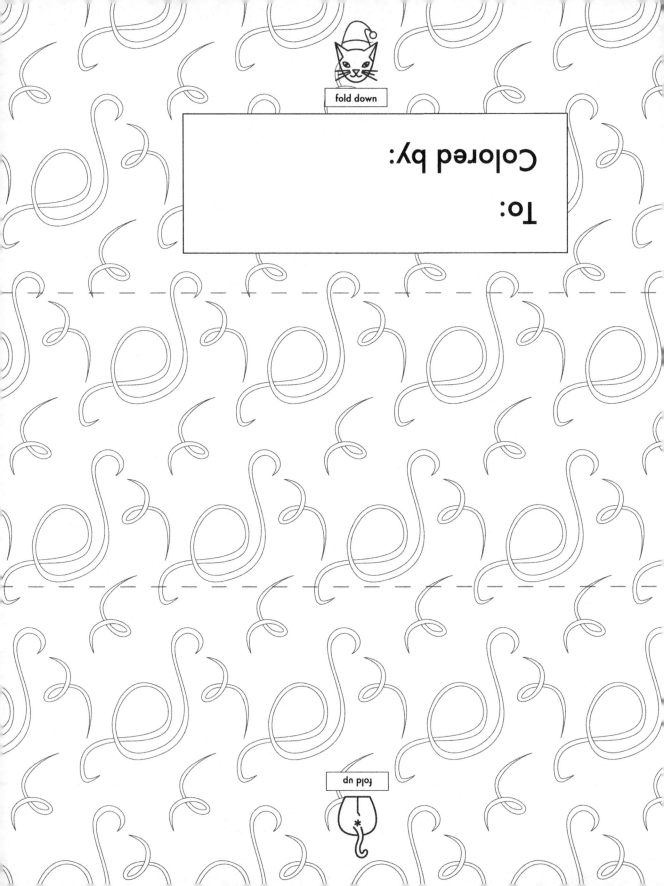

fold down

Colored by:

To:

fold up

MINTY FRESH CAT BUTT

fold down

Colored by:

To:

fold up

SANTA SALUTATION

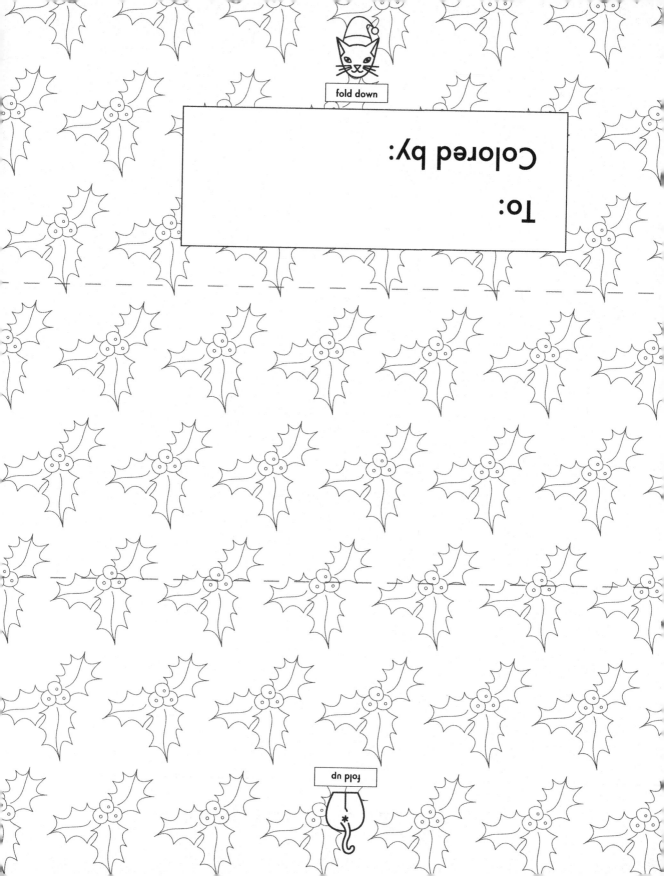

fold down

Colored by:

To:

fold up

CHOCOLATE BUTTSTACHE

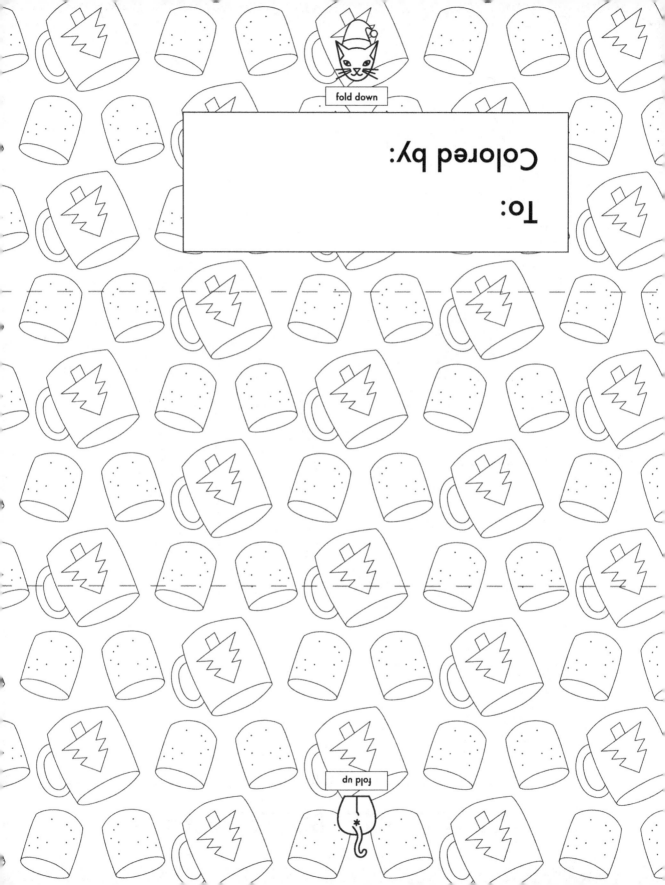

fold down

To:

Colored by:

fold up

CRAFTY CAT BUTT

fold down

Colored by:

To:

fold up

JINGLE BUTTS

fold down

Colored by:

To:

fold up

TRIPLE CRACKXEL

fold down

Colored by:

To:

fold up

SEE INTO THE POOTURE

fold down

To:

Colored by:

fold up

STOCKING STUFFER

fold down

To: Colored by:

fold up

OH WREATHLY

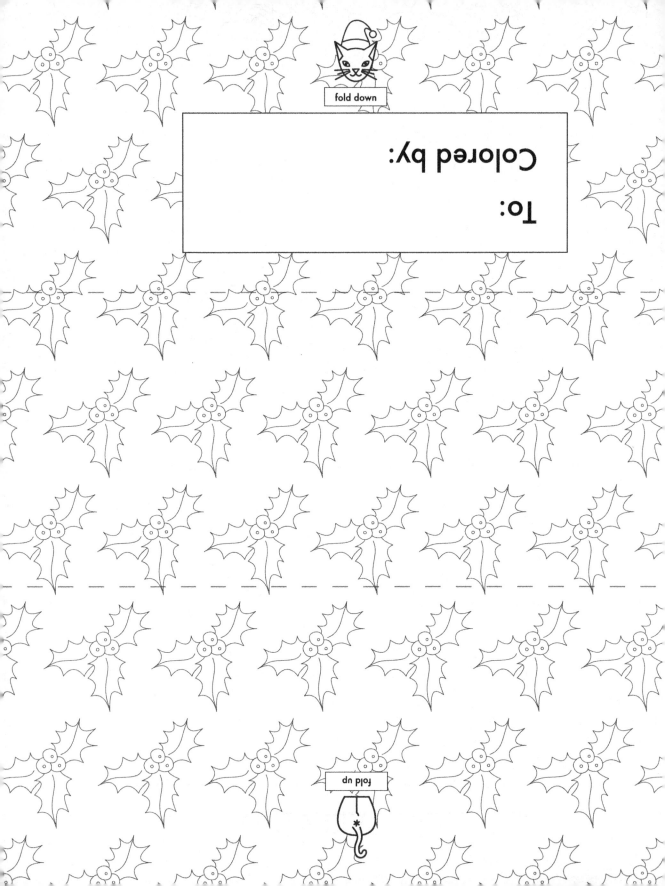

fold down

To: Colored by:

fold up

PICKLE PANIC

fold down

To: Colored by:

fold up

ILLUMINATING PERSPECTIVE

fold down

Colored by:

To:

fold up

CAT BUTT BY THE FIRE

fold down

Colored by:

To:

fold up

THE BUTTCRACKER

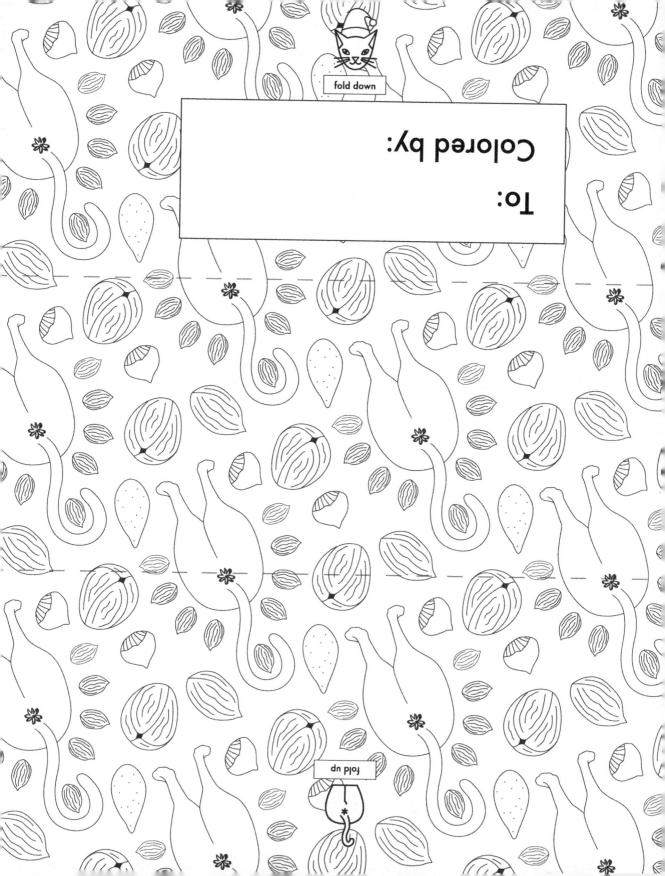

fold down

To:

Colored by:

fold up

CAT BUTT CONSTRUCTION

fold down

To:

Colored by:

fold up

A
CAT BUTT CHRISTMAS
HAIKU

Christmas is jolly
When you've got lots of cat butts
Stuffing your stocking

#icoloredcatbutts   #catbuttcoloringbook   @catbuttcoloring

Thank you for reading!

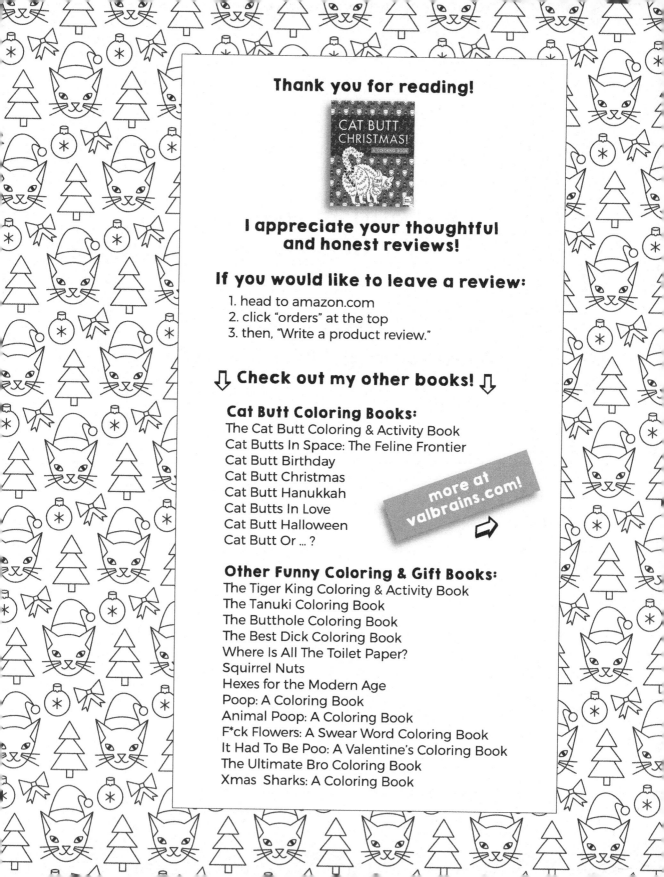

CAT BUTT CHRISTMAS!
A COLORING BOOK

I appreciate your thoughtful and honest reviews!

If you would like to leave a review:

1. head to amazon.com
2. click "orders" at the top
3. then, "Write a product review."

⇩ Check out my other books! ⇩

Cat Butt Coloring Books:
The Cat Butt Coloring & Activity Book
Cat Butts In Space: The Feline Frontier
Cat Butt Birthday
Cat Butt Christmas
Cat Butt Hanukkah
Cat Butts In Love
Cat Butt Halloween
Cat Butt Or … ?

more at valbrains.com! ➡

Other Funny Coloring & Gift Books:
The Tiger King Coloring & Activity Book
The Tanuki Coloring Book
The Butthole Coloring Book
The Best Dick Coloring Book
Where Is All The Toilet Paper?
Squirrel Nuts
Hexes for the Modern Age
Poop: A Coloring Book
Animal Poop: A Coloring Book
F*ck Flowers: A Swear Word Coloring Book
It Had To Be Poo: A Valentine's Coloring Book
The Ultimate Bro Coloring Book
Xmas Sharks: A Coloring Book

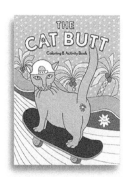

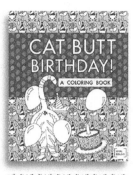

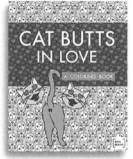

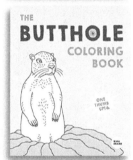

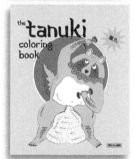

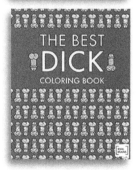

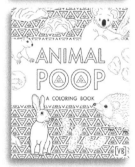

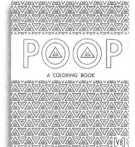

Made in the USA
Monee, IL
10 December 2020